Self-evident

Self-evident

Scott Hightower

Barrow Street Press
New York City

Designed by Robert Drummond

Cover photography by Mark Morrisroe. © The Estate of Mark
Morrisroe (Ringier Collection) at Fotomuseum Winterthur.
     "Self-Portrait With Broken Finger, Christmas 1984"
     Mark Morrisroe
     C-print, negative sandwich
     1984

Published by Barrow Street Press
Distributed by:
     Barrow Street Books
     P.O. Box 1558
     Kingston, RI 02881

First Edition

Library of Congress Control Number: 2012930851

ISBN 978-0-9819876-6-8

For Sofia and Diego

CONTENTS

Infant Gods

Reading : Writing

The uniformed, white-tipped coal lump bodies
of the grazing geese float with a constancy
on the fixed parade field of snow. Their heads
and feet dip with mechanical reptilian grace.
On snow days, we keep our eyes down:
sand, smudged cement, and gravel. And there
it is—the aesthetically charged abstract
placeholder, the world floating in a world.

"Self-evident"

Jefferson penned, "We
hold these truths to be..."
and sent off the draft to Franklin,
his colleague, who in turn
crossed out and penned
over the word "sacred."

•

In silk stockings and a suit
tailored in the style of the day,
he looks like a lean figurine

marked "Made in Occupied
Japan." Except he
is a real man in a full suit

of fine blue satin.
His skills more readily
fit with pen and well

than the public stage
of indignant declamation.
His scholarship flourishes

down the page from oppositional
claims to fuse of self-determination,
bouquet of checks and balances.

He, of course, would have had
Shakespeare's dramatic soliloquies,
but not the seclusions of Dickinson.

And the unfurling truths of the Bible,
but not the orations of Whitman.
No Darwin, no Freud.

In a landscape anticipated
by the philosophy of liberty,
the news unfolds incrementally

into new intimacies, new
dignities, new spells of rest.
A new song of emancipation

and continuity rises
'midst the sovereignties
of sweet accumulation.

Walking at the U.N.

This afternoon, I visit a friend,
a deputy of the European Commission.
We walk in the U.N. rose garden.
Last time I was here, it was open
to the public. (He explains since Sept. 11th,

the garden has only been accessible
to U.N. employees and their guests.)
The sun burns like a wick in our conversation
and, later, in the unpredictable current of the river.
How from island to island people bound in nations

find their way, even as the unparsed narratives
of the conquered and vanquished more often
fall away. "In the presence of my enemy."
You are a slick scalawag to my American
parched corn, but we both have read our

Paine, and "malice" is not a binder
or a virtue in our shared rubric. Writing—
more specifically Poetry—lies at the elemental
core of democracy. By definition, *it seeks a foundation
for the commonwealth in the truth*

*of the individual, guaranteed and restored
through the integrity of language.*
New poets stand in the midst of old stones,
envisioning new ways, are, after all,
themselves part of this tallow world.

Imperial Carpet

"Like Red Riding Hood looking
for a cuddle in the wolf's bed."
Arundhati Roy

What do I know about this place . . .
real comfort . . . design . . . anything?

I write JUSTICE • DECENCY • FAIR PLAY
and throw them with the meat
into the old mechanical grinder.
In some houses the *bloody*
grinder is sleek and new;
in some, it's clunky,
pitted, and traditional.

On another piece of paper
I write: LOVE IS
A COLLABORATIVE ART.
It gets tossed in, too.

Once, I even mixed "green" cow
dung with Knowledge and Need
and kerosene . . . and crafted the glop
into a clay. When it dried,
I was grateful for its unglamorous
comfort stretching like paper
across a concrete floor.

"The Persians" By Ellen Mclaughlin
(The National Actors Theater 2003 NYC Production)

What some of the watchers will come
to know . . . some of the characters,
locked in the hermetics of the play,

will never be burdened with.
The landscape of ambivalence
is vast . . . vast as a nation.

All through it, *WHY* spread
around beneath the actors' feet
like light-smeared red sand . . .

with a ghostly purple backlight
and a tilted mirror
over far upstage—

where tradition would
have had a faint sky
above a tomb—

and the infinities
of individuals
with uncertainties billowing

like a censer swinging in great arcs
across a stone transept.
The present and the past

inherit each other.
This is today's snap
of reaper take all.

In the end, *the black
garland of victory and woe*
belongs only to the audience.

Beauty

is one of the greatest mysteries of nature.

•

Every day a pressure rises,
brutalities brew;

the pure in spirit are tried
as they accommodate

the mechanical demands
of the physical, repetitive world.

Repetition for Divinity is myth;
repetition for mortals is labor.

"Row, row,
row your boat."

•

Jonah in the belly
of the great fish

The avatars of prophecy and the institutionalization
of wisdom: oracle, sibyl, sage, book

The horses over
the doors of San Marco

The idea of a physical,
noble Greek antiquity

The French Revolution
cutting off the head of a king

The Mechanical Revolution
Skyscrapers

Assembly Lines
The Panopticon

•

With "imitation" one does not mean
slavish copying. . . . "What is imitated,
if handled with reason,
may assume another nature,
as it were, and becomes one's own."

Johann Winckelmann, a genius
who offered a paradigm:
that "noble simplicity
and quiet grandeur" might once
have changed the way

we viewed and organized
ourselves and others in the world.
Not a small order: moving realms,
giving the ideological
wheel of the world a little turn!

Backwards. Forwards.
Poor Winckelmann. So able.
So civilized. Dogged by loneliness.
Stabbed by a hotel acquaintance
and dying in Trieste at 51.

Platée

1.
Expedient, baroque entertainment
for a young bride born in the Escorial: 1745.

Within a year, her July death will be recorded
by a royal attendant with a flourish
in the residence of Versailles.

                    A couple of years
beyond the extravagant nuptial gavotting,
and, likewise, her daughter will be recorded
and laid by her side.

"How delicate the equipoise."

2.
The shepherds—archaic or modern—
at their watering hole,
and the smaller creatures—
moist and brief:

all of them sipping from a great bowl.

And the race of the immortals,
uniformed frequent fliers, absolute
and radiant in their gold and white,
tinkle the ice in their drinks
in the sky's perpetual cocktail party.

Once you exist, your divinity exists
untarnished forever, even after
the last supplicant, the last devotee,
dies—cruelly lapsing you
into oblivion. And yet,
"Tis very tedious, this respect."

A capricious quartet of cloven-footed
satyrs are dressed in nipple rings
and revealing black leather jock straps.
They spank one another into a frenzy.

Living beyond every phoenix, you too
surely would take to the haute couture
beyond Mycenaean gutta percha
and the elite ante-modern black anodyne dye.

The director and costume designer
have updated the colorful capers
and illuminations. A showgirl in bridal white.

The brave and bright-eyed French tenor
channels the vanity and pathos of the naiad queen.
She stands awkwardly at the apex of the scene—
and edge of the dish—like a fabulous,
green gorilla doomed by her own nature.

3.
In the darkness, ancient human
motives effervesce apart . . .
and then stubbornly begin coalescing again.

Yet everywhere the abundance
of the fascinating temporal: lightning
cracking through the crown of a violet sky;
fire, fireworks, rainbows, and rivers;
the aurora, the moon and stars; courage
and vision; an eagle, a fish, a polar bear,
a porpoise, a blue bird, a doe-eyed dog,
a set of baby ducks, a set of baby tigers;
ocean waves; grasshoppers; clouds;
cherry blossoms; clean water; silly
human affections; noble human
affections; salamanders;

measured and unmeasured time.

Le Soldat Avec Les Besoins Infantiles

Ah, "Genie out of the Bottle,
Egyptian among the Bulrushes,
Cocktail Naiad among the Cattails,"

his assumptions flamed transportive,
heroic, and bright: after one night . . .
after one spell . . . after one spill

down the rabbit hole, lucky him.
Girlfriend, you were going to be
his ticket, his endless cradle of luck!

The rest of his days, I was going
to be whipping up wild honey
and *cinguale* after hustling home

the proverbial bacon? I don't think so!
Actually, he wants a mother!
Would that he could parse his own

infantile fantasy with a bit more insight
rather than cauterize the genuine
intimacy we might have found together.

Him going on about his "hog," his guns,
how none of his buddies were hippy dippy,
his own latent willingness to one day

crack open "The Joy of Cooking"
or develop some interest in a worthy
handicraft—leather-work, shoeing

horses, gardening. . . macramé.
On and on, and all the time it
being just a racy one-night stand!

Mon Dieu! Afterwards, I knew
he would resort to grumbling
from some perverse shadow

of his own masochistic imagination,
that there would be a dramatic
monologue about being abandoned.

Would that he grasped that each
of us does well but to serve up
to the other the most ordinary joy!

The whole undulating world
is complete and florid,
is a single rhapsodic

motion. And, as you
and I well know—his
own gorgeous, archaic

whiny self-indulgence
included—everywhere, there
are sweet songs worth singing;

there are sad songs to listen to.
Everywhere, there are songs,
songs, songs: beautiful songs.

Noblesse Oblige, Before the Mirror

> "Your passion would invent a thousand sophisms
> to justify your love"
> Bellino to Casanova

Toys have long borrowed their shape
from those of weapons. Some irony,

that today many improvised
explosive devices take their innards

from electronic toys. A friend,
a live wire fop fully aware

of the banality of nobility,
used to claim the only

thing he had to declare
at customs was his heart.

•

Once, physically, there might have been
the finery of a black riding coat,

a retinue of fans and sparkling jewels,
and a gold-trimmed green canopy of silk

not far from the laden table of the Duke
of Parma. The most spectacular explosions

of the evening might have been abstract: poet
artfully dueling poet, like Casanova, himself,

at the table with Henriette—who, like her host,
the Duke—did not take sugar in her coffee.

Casanova's record of the evening shares
that, except for Henriette, the gathering

was only of *pavos reales* and *paons*,
a setting composed for the glib postures

of the dilettante Duke to keep
sending his spells and inventions

up against Casanova's authentic attempts
at clarity. At one point when Henriette referred

to the accommodating position the cello demanded,
Casanova noted, "While the Spaniards bit their lips,

the Frenchmen roared with laughter."
Given, to some, Casanova, too, might have been

a bit comical, always waxing so . . . philosophical
(Poetry as the custodian of one's honor.

Ugh!). He did have a performative sense
(magic, fashion, religion). Had a sartorial eye

for theater, regarded the mysterious,
evoked courtesy and ceremony,

dabbled in the sciences in his reach
for the unknown. "Rome,

if I were a woman . . . ,"
stridently putting himself up

against the Vulgar—never equating
carnal pleasure with sin.

In good time, this artful philanderer
with no revolutionary ardor

would survive terrible translations
(there is another story there)

to become one of the great journalists
of the golden age Europe.

Having bathed in a canvas-draped
wooden tub, he attires himself

in a—magenta? chartreuse? periwinkle?
black? yes, his stately and very expensive—

black *redingote* (that flashes
with every gesture its crystal buttons)

and dons one of his finest wigs
before a lent mirror: Steed,

dude, attuned to Virgil, Ovid,
Petrarch, and Dante's stars.

Orfeo ed Euridice

(The Metropolitan Opera, 2009)

"Till Death do we part."
One is left with the razor,

the brush, the soap, the closet
to empty. We wind off into the city

to catch Mark Morris's production
of Gluck's "Orfeo ed Euridice."

Those no longer walking in sunlight
are shelved like spices in three

very tall racks. Living eyes,
free to choose their focus on the stage,

move amiably about the historical characters'
costumes. The chorus is classically grand,

their gestures casually synchronized,
sitting or standing, each carefully

embodying the place the procession ends.
As this is art that knows it is art,

winged Love, sporting running shoes
and a subtly bejeweled

pink polo shirt, descends
by wires. (The tiny stones

in Love's shirt divinely flicker
and twinkle.) After the theatrics

of passion and loss, Death
spiritedly rewinds Euridice up to Orfeo

like a Jean Cocteau movie scene
run in reverse. The gears of shepherds

and nymphs folk dancing in the sunlight
are colorful, joyous, and restorative.

They sparkle a bit—like the strap
of Orfeo's guitar, which Love takes up.

Every year reliving the anniversary
of the August fifth news

of Marilyn Monroe's death,
"Who Killed Norma Jean"

unfurls itself in my head.
Today, July twenty-third,

the devastating
news is of Amy Winehouse.

the heart wants what the heart
wants what the heart wants

Franklin in Paris

Wily diplomat, Protestant in a modest
frock and a Catholic country. It takes
a month for news to come. Meanwhile,
you borrow, bargain, buy, and ship
in French. You wine and dine
and assess the right horse to bet on.
Your own stock is high. You remain
optimistic about the diplomatic
sacrifice of aristocratic laughter
and luxury. You wait and watch
for a break. Death waits. The Champs Elysée
and wide avenues of Paris wait.
Two World Wars wait. The twin towers
of the World Trade Center wait.
I think you might have a different take
on "arms for hostages," the UN,
"water-boarding" and "zip ties,"
NATO, "weapons of mass destruction,"
the Twenty-First Century treaty
establishing a constitution
for democratic Europe and North America,
Islamic governments trying
to find their way into modernity,
China rocketing into the fray.

That Which Is Committed to Thy Trust

Previously, radiant displays and their reflections
had played off surfaces with a marvelous
lightness. Only rarely had there been
a hint of the less amusing chemistry
and terror ahead: a blackballing
and the subsequent reprisal,
someone pouring boiling water
on someone else's best roses,
Marat's bath.

Madame Lavoisier knows how scientific knowledge
eats at the table. How freedom of inquiry
sleeps. How in times of permissiveness
it drinks and dances. How it grows a different garden,
mixes a new drink, dispatches a new remedy,
recharges its own tongue by listening to how idioms
give themselves up in other languages' humorous translations.

Madame Lavoisier can draw. She can
foresee new inquiries, the classification
of new elements. What she cannot do
is protect her father or her
husband from the game afoot,
a malicious line of reasoning
that ends only at "the scaffold of justice."

But, even in homes where knowledge dreams,
any warrant of the state is an absolute in a turbulent time.

Patriotic clubs and new masses of power elites
are not always a friend to inquiry . . . are not always
a friend to the motives of liberty and reason . . .

are not always decent or fair to those who have opened up
a different kind of space in their lives for knowledge.

Later, she will silently study the suspended,
palms, the tender neck and breasts,
the unstockinged extended leg
of one of Jacques-Louis's Sabine women.

Noble Chart, A Radiance – 1794
("Monsieur Lavoisier and his Wife," Jacques-Louis David,
   1788, The Metropolitan Museum of Art)

It is the morning of May eighth;
Madame Lavoisier has just been
orphaned. Within a few more minutes
she, likewise, will be widowed,

the guillotine, oddly taking the name
of a man who did not invent it.

May eighth thus invests itself,
not in the talent of one
of Jacques-Louis David's
death warrants,
but in one set of his details,
which, today, beyond heroic,
feels meaningful and human:

a full white dress, a soft, luminous mass,
a cascade of curls, the elegant pale blue
bow and sash, and the oddly
prophetic red velvet tablecloth.
The felicity of the shoe buckle and—
like a fine glass instrument in
a laboratory—the black silk stocking
covering Lavoisier's extended leg
take on a luster from hues around them.

With a quill scratch,
Aristotle's essences give way
to the emerging periodic table.
An example of what to do
with knowledge
if, indeed, it is the stuff
that actually makes us human.

In the next five years, the orderly
radiance will dissimulate
into the cruel fragrance of ideals!

The noble privilege of cataloging observations
will succumb to the emerging urgency
of the next elemental question,

"Who bears witness to the shimmering
unreason of this most deplorable single casualty?"

"Never forget; never forgive," the dark
precision of the glinting tooth of class
and counter-class spellbounds.
The familiar weapon once used
for attack drops. "There
is no defense."

Where is the beauty that hallowed
Death has erased so quickly
with the tip of his wing?

"One Arm"
("Self Portrait with Broken Finger, Christmas 1984"
Mark Morrisroe)

This is the season Tennessee
Williams' "One Arm"
comes to the New York summer stage
on the heels of a Mark Morrisroe photograph
exhibition.
               Serge Neville's shot
of Claybourne Elder—blue, toned
to a grainy cyan-green—
shows the lead publicly photographed
for playbill and postcards.

The glow of the boxer's salty skin
is cold: the milk of grain and the milk
and grain of marble. Slight blush
of pink and dove above hustling's hard edges.
A teal Caravaggio with sparring glove
instead of Morrisroe's soft-wrap cast.

Another Lear, odd taste of decline and increase . . .
shelter denied is its own degradation.

When love proves transient
or is refused, brutality hosts.

The surrender diminishing us into desire,
elusively, is the self-same that raises us up.

All Gussied Up in Prague

Unfortunately, tomorrow we won't be seeing
the white Spanish Hall in the Bishop's Palace.
Though we've studied photographs of it
reproduced in pages of web and books,
the thing itself is not opened to tourists.

At the end of our visit at the far reaches
of the palace, we'll consider torture.
It's desire, fear, and sadism gussied up
and rationalized as justice—no matter who
the desperate subjects might have appealed to:
Elizabeth, Barbara, George, Mary, Jesus,
or Allah. Torture's current incarnation
seems to be . . . gussied up for tourism:
a fleece for a rug and an empty bowl
in each of the bulging, makeshift cells
opened to the elements on the edges
of this chilly tower. What songs
weren't heard here between the deer
ravine and the soldier's quarters,
in this vertical bowl far from god or king?
At first, the hearth grate seems little more
than a grill to warm a meal. Awful
these vestiges and real ghosts.

Piercing black-roofed towers' amber
glows high in the night. Cavaradossi
would like the present wacky, lovely facades,
would enjoy super titles and the shadowy
Svoboda sets; Angelotti, a grilled Easter *klobasa*
and hand-picked strawberries from Huelva.
Above arching *mosti*, the sky mirrors stars
thrown back and caught in the weir's churn.
Marionettes, instruments, translations . . . .
Carried by the current, "Carlos" bleeds
into "Charlie" or "Karlov"—and back.

Passing Through the Corridor

The mechanical ventilation hoods
of New Haven bow
in silhouette against fading

orange and blue swerves.
Fringes of winter trees, overhead,
reach like dark vessels.

Many of my friends seem
to prefer the melodrama
of David & Jonathan.

Must be something bucolic
ingrained in the inner landscape.
The metropolitan edge

is clearly David & Saul,
tragic and operatic melody
up against malice, each note

connected by the inevitable
beat that follows a king's,
a tyrant's, or a giant's fall.

The Zeppelin Field at Nürnberg

Rollerbladers cocooned
in earphones occupy the site.

A photographer busily shoots
a lanky, posing model

sporting a clear and extravagant
tattoo. I shoot them

from overhead, from the platform
where the Führer

and his industrious cronies stood
and spoke, were photographed.

A creative break from my own
taking in of the expansive scale.

Like miniature, the imagination
creates vastness. Millions

snapped their crisp salutes
like guillotines. The result

of the romantic
madness still hangs

profound and murderous
in the air: train cars, camps,

sequentialing tattoos, gas,
and reels of propaganda. I watch

swans gliding and dipping between
the dark silhouettes of trunks.

The sky and pond are
opalescent. Hardly concealed

systemic cruelty contains
the urban Turkish neighborhoods

not far away. Let the concrete edges
of this field continue to crumble.

We're thirsty. Time to drive back
to the power station building—

source of light, to make
transparent part of what it was

that was being ambitiously
designed, stoked, and rallied.

I will cajole someone to take
a series of photographs of me

posing outside the converted
plant. Me: sated, victorious

and mocking, a ridiculous,
cheesy pin-up model—

the latest to strut and plug
for the kingdom of fast food.

The Bath Scene in "Gattopardo"

"... being yourselves also in the body."
Hebrews 13:3

Time enough for the allegorical waltz
(the time-honed aristocracy—on Fabrizio,

giving the new coifed nation in its
dazzling gown a turn about the floor),

the pensive face (an expression
not as easily cast off as a garment)

searching in the painting or the mirror—
nearby, all the elegant chamber pots

full of the bodies' corrupted waters
(ancestral step—biological, literary,

cinematographic, photographic—
toward Andres Serrano's "Piss Christ")

and the private humble prayer:
"Please, give me profound strength

that I may reach—
as I sincerely believe

once promised to me
in a time

before these times—
a place of less inconstancy

(one nervous breakdown,
two posthumous novels)."

This is the scene where
the fretful man of the cloth

faces—without modesty
or malice—the man gracefully

toweling off, the latter's declining
body supporting the private burden

of a just, ante-modern soul
(the glistening Lancaster, Visconti,

the melancholic Don Fabrizio,
Tomasi, the Prince of Lampedusa).

Royalties

"Una terribile tosse l'esil petto le scuote..."
Rodolfo

Even though I have seen first-rate
productions, have heard remarkable voices

offer up its undeniably beautiful songs,
and even though its philosophical themes

are noble in their humanity, I have never
felt very compelled by "La Boheme."

I appreciate that after the French Revolution
the lives of philosophers and artists in Paris

became harder than in lands where kings
were allowed to keep their heads.

After the Revolution, many
who were previously well fed

came to know hunger. "Te lo rammenti
quando sono entrata la prima volta, la?"

is a line worthy of an Eve browsing
in the place that used to be a paradise.

With or without revolutions,
one comes to one's own death.

Mimi begins the sentence alone,
"Soli . . . ." But she and Rodolfo

complete the line together,
". . . d'inverno é cosa da morire!"

Liu's Executioner

Again, the rustling curtains of the palace
are parted with the scent of hope eliding
into a cone of uncertainty. The noise
of industry penetrates every shadow.
Over and over, he responds
to the summons. Though, this time,
the fugitive heart of the implication
is that of a young foreign woman.

He wears two wide leather wristbands,
a leather belt, and a resplendent
magenta skirt. Large pink tears—
or are they the prints of curled edges of fists? —
bend in the voluminous folds. A hem
of gold fringe hovers at his bare feet.

In the eerie moonlight, his
swarthy arms, neck, and chest reveal
acquired athletic definition.

A snarling demon mask covers—
and, later, uncovers—his face.
Odd, to see it exposed here, upstage,
on the terrace of a royal garden.

Many times, I've tossed
a furtive glance his way
in the gym, a quisitive taking,
in consideration of his deafness.
The stage lights dim. Wrapped.

The stage lights dim. We all
stand, unable to escape
the grandeur of Liu's exit.

Serai

The palace is riddled with sounds;
a kiss of reason wings

through each bureaucrat's silence,
a world at stake

in the wealth
of each jester's gesture.

Like the Buddhist icons
and Hindu dancers

with their mudras
before (and after) them,

the mute attendants of the seraglio
engage in a purity of gesticulations:

the duplicity of a scrotum grab,
the strangulating bow string,

what it means to be taken
without a prayer.

Dixie Queen

Tennessee Williams knew how
to mine the kinetics of cruelty.

Not the inverted and demure,
"I'll roll over, and let you

ravish me, you he-man man, you!"
Forget Stella. No. It's Stanley,

the shrieking infantile god,
who's vicious, who's had enough

of just "whistling Dixie,"
who finally succumbs

to being topped
by Stella's transvestite

brother, who, in turn,
has had enough

of railroad Johns,
and of turning

hotel tricks
in the magical

and occupying
glow of paper

and red glass
lanterns.

The Afternoons of Infant Gods

The usual object of Baby Jesus's affection
is Mary, though that same affection
seems more charged than simply
that of a son for his mother.
The currency seems less modest,
more of a husband about to kiss his bride.

Case in point: Cambiaso's holy child.
In the painting, the boy
is impish and determined
and the coy Madonna turns her head
to the right. A boy who—and I suggest
this in reverence and not ribaldry—
in a few more years, will be a loaded
teenager clumsily fondling
or himself being groped.

•

If I drag my lips along your skin
after a little commingling,
is it really rational?

•

In the original, Peter Pan kisses
Wendy. Unlike many a baby
captured in a Renaissance
painting, Peter is always
and only a son reverently
giving his mother a kiss.

Peter Llewelyn-Davies emotionally
wrestled under the conditions
of Uncle Jimmy's overheated
attentiveness and his terrible
—and in the end—unbearable
masterpiece for nearly 60 years.

And then dismembered
California angels so ruthlessly
dusted private intentions
from "Finding Neverland"
that nowhere in the film
is there a single kiss.

Lately, Opening the Refrigerator

has become enough, in itself, to cause me
to spin into decline, "lose heart":

my brother, my closest friend,
friends that illness emasculated
until they could not
keep up the fight. Thrush.
Kaposi's sarcoma. Lesions.
Pneumonia. Self-consciousness.

Found. Their notion of rage
and complete despair.

•

We sit in the Presidential box
of the Prague opera house and twitter
our observations of the opulence
of the theater, Mozart,

and the affordability
of the outstanding production
of "Tosca" with the descant
of a brilliant bass (presented
as a revolutionary slav)
tortured just the night before.

Tonight's stage is lavish with flaneurs,
vibrant singers, and historical Parisian cutouts.

The opera—which has never before
really quite worked for me—
opens and closes in a garret,
two despairing choruses:

a group of grieving women,

a line of men lending
support to one another,

these broken things
of this world, this shelter.

Lutece

We are just a couple of centuries past the sillion
of the pagan empire of empires. Tonight there
are issues of succession in North Korea and lethal
skirmishes of partisans in Syria. Haredi men
in Israel are spitting on one of their own preteen
girls for not dressing modestly enough
for their flashpoint dictates. And contagious
violence has broken out at a celebrated mall
in the United States. Joyeux Noël!
Lovely Cecilia Gallerani cuddling
her white stoat might as well have been
a Huguenot innocently nestling
eighty-three years later in the arms
of her lover. Thirty thousand killed . . .
and an amnesty to pardon the perpetrators.

And then there is the story of weaponizing H5N1;
like Jules Leotard, it now "swings through the air
with the greatest of ease": lab ferrets
with the mutated bird virus traveling
through the air between their scrupulously
labeled cages. *Lutetia non urbus, sed orbis.*
Whether it is out of lethal intolerance,
desire, or ineptitude, it may all
come down to the same consequence.

Infidelity, like syphilis, might emerge briefly—
like a saboteur—and then appear to vanish:
the king infected by a targeted consort
or an unfaithful liaison. Such
are the possible mutations of love.

Some gray matter, a garter, a child's heart;
a fontange—not a "Belle Poule"—but still
grand, a tiarra of dried rose stems and paste,
the skull of a once elegant woman.

It's nearing Christmas and—though not ourselves
cephalophores—like others before us,
we've found our way here. We are tourists—
not pilgrims. We're scientific, partisan,
and as dubious about valor of suffering as we are
about any notion of magic transferred through blood.

Entering St. Denis, I pick up a copy of "Kings of France
and Their Wives" at the abbey souvenir stand.
It does appear transport made some boatmen
rich on winding rivers before they silted up,
before they had their religious stones carted off
to another bank to anchor a museum. Inheritance
without love and affection? I'm not any surer
about bequeathed family legacies: there's
a lot of hokum and lots of rancor over wampum.

Under blinking holiday lights tonight Ava Jane
and Jay will play with rented bumper cars
on a rented track on the Champs d'Elysee.
Some clever local businessman will earn
a few euro and we will take pictures.

At Malmaison

She could consider the cedar,
a celebration of one of his imperial

victories, every day from her window.
It has outlived them, the decorum

of their love, some of their
promises and dreams. Today

a ways down the lane before
the caliche and the guard gate,

one can find a sustaining lunch
at "The Pavilion Josephine." Clumsy

and concealing, the Malmaison
site attendants are English caricatures

of French rudeness, and the parterres
of roses—once reported

as amazing—"dazzling in their array"—
are modest and have gone to weed.

Imagine the gravel crunching
beneath Napoleon's tread

after Marengo. Rose resting,
enlivened, considering some nuance

of the slate roof, the transplanted
cedar from her half-opened

window, some notion of
shelter, some notion of home.

Brújula (Rose Of Exile)

. . . Tu lascerai ogne cosa diletta
più caramente; e questo è quello strale
che l'arco de lo essilio pria saetta.
Tu proverai sì come sa di sale
lo pane altrui, e come è duro calle
lo scendere e 'l salir per l'altrui scale . . .

". . . You shall leave everything you love most:
this is the arrow that the bow of exile
shoots first. You are to know the bitter taste
of others' bread, how salty it is, and know
how hard a path it is for one who goes
ascending and descending others' stairs . . ."

—Dante "The Paradiso," Canto XVII, lines 58 to 63

Plaza de la Encarnación, Seville

(Horacio Hermoso Araujo, d. 1936)

Here kingdoms have been razed
and ransomed, often starting
with a disguise, a pair
of eyes, a mother's love,
a radiating spot of blood.

The same yellow flowers
that elsewhere have long spelled out
"Where is the grave of Virgil?"
here, in March, volunteer
across Roman excavations.
Sometimes their text gasps,
"Why have you forsaken me?"
Other times, it jubilates,
"You have not abandoned me!"

But not one of the three sunlit palms
blooming today in the square—
not one of the three
giant, green carnations
opening like a secret heart—
gives up the final words
or location of the mustard-
covered grave of Horacio Hermoso,
the last elected Republican mayor of Seville.

"Era un Maricón"

"There's a tree where the doves go to die…
There's a bar where the boys have stopped talking
They've been sentenced to death by the blues."
Leonard Cohen, "Take this Waltz"
after Federico García-Lorca's
"Little Viennese Waltz"

Many books on the great Andalucían
poet mention that his brother-in-law,
the Republican mayor of Granada
was assassinated. What is less
often stated is that Granada had
had no mayor for many months,
because the city was so
disturbed, no one dared
to accept the dangerous position.
When Montesinos accepted it,
he was killed within ten days.

One morning, that summer, Conchita,
Federico García-Lorca's sister,
lost her thirty-five-year-old husband
—father of her children,
physician, politician—
to the malice of a mechanical death.

*(There's a piece that was torn from the morning
and it hangs in the Gallery of Frost.)*

Three days later, she would lose
her phenomenally talented
thirty-eight-year-old brother.

Federico's books were burned
in Granada's Plaza del Carmen
and were soon banned from Franco's Spain.

"Where does the body of our sweet
brother Federico García-Lorca rest?"

Conchita Montesinos died
in a car accident
thirteen years before Franco,
the press only noting,
"A woman died today."

The dossier regarding Federico's death,
compiled at Franco's request,
has yet to surface.

But even before the terrible war had started
García-Lorca had already had the last word:
I will leave my mouth between your legs.

Victoria Kent

The whole time you work away
—both the physical Soldat

and the fantastic La Belle Dame Avec Merci—
the sudarium is safely locked away

in Oviedo. Throughout your land,
there is blood on the ground

and trouble at the heart of the tree.
You hang framed prints of sowers

and gleaners (Millet's, Van Gogh's,
or another's) on your wall.

(A few of the prison reforms
you wrestled into implementation

in Madrid will take root
in the rest of the world:

prisoners, allowed home visits;
the ball and chain cruelty

will be relegated to cartoons.)
You and like-minded others

try to get out the word: "Freedom
has to be plucked from yourself

in silence and in darkness."
You and some of the others

will soon seek solace
by ambling flea markets,

will come to the tasting of salt
on the bread of other lands,

will come to know too well
that—between the dream

and the physical routine
of the day—a barrage of obedient

and rewarded representatives
of those who consider

themselves "more
gifted in taking charge"

will be happy to barge in
and seize the fleece, the day

in the middle of the night,
the bull by the horns.

At Every "Tosca"

Tosca and Scarpia are in the wings,
warming up for their bout of tussling.
The woman in charge of props

has decanted "the Spanish wine,"
located the silver knife with a spring,
and, for the opening act,

has placed an apple
in the artist's lunchbox
beside his paint box.

The literal fate of a Roman revolutionary
(*consul of a failed republic*),
though sealed offstage,

eventually, will be spit out on cue
by a messenger of the regime.
What actually becomes of him

may not be any clearer
than what became
of *the Head of the Republic*

of Spain in Exile. What little I know
has come to me over a glass
of wine, which is to say,

via vague de Albornoz family stories
of the promising, exiled generations
of Álvaro persisting in Mexico after Paris.

There Are Lecagies Beyond Land

Luarca: long lean landscape of beautiful gray
sky * port and beaches of rugged sea bluff
and ocean-washed stone * inheritance
that stretches out like damp cotton sheets *
Celtic touched Bable: foreign struggle, odd
to my insensitive Teutonic ears and tongue.
"Bruxo": "brujo" be gone! You feed me,
actually, have fed my American mother
the delicacies of your tradition,

those that sustain me (my in-law Spanish family)
were awake when the military cargo trucks
came through the streets. The gentle father
of a playmate waved. And was gone.
The light trucks undemocratically
carted the familiar friend up
to the pockmarked cemetery wall.
Young modest widows, here, have wept
at the windows of their apartments
for years.
        Men that go down to the sea vote
white stone, black stone. Even the widows
of those lost cast a stone. Decency, democratic
principles, and rugged self-reliance lives
in the fishing villages and small mining towns
of northern Spain. Luarca, tough, resilient,
and grounded, I came to your granaries
and lanes a bride, with only the dowry
of poetry, my sophistication green.

A Life Facing the Sea

(Severo Ochoa, 1905-1993)

I've gotten used to the exceeded expectations
of the perfumed and well-bred. Tonight,
the bread is not warm and the drinks are stirred,
not shaken. But, at a point, even the flickering
legacy of pedigree is no longer about poverty
or prosperity. One's hold on much of the physical
world is provisional . . . like merriment.
Or even better, like the past, simultaneously
active and potential, more or less always resting,
waiting to be claimed—like a wineglass
turned down on the table waiting to be taken up.

•

> "I know who I am
> and who I may be, if I choose."
> Miguel de Cervantes Saavedra

The cricket in the boy's cage
has been put away and he re-enters
the world of negotiated reconciliations.
Next year, the lad's mother—
a descendent from the family
of a cardinal—will put on a black dress
and pack away personal things.
She and the boy will leave Villar
and go to Málaga and the Mediterranean Sea.
The stately neo-Gothic house with its high windows,
servant's quarters, and chapel; the vast
garden with its stone fences, fountain, benches,
and statues (when you took me there,
was it my imagination that you hummed
"Platée?"), the gusty Atlantic winds,
the beautiful cliffs and stony beaches
would not fit into a humpback steamer trunk.

Walking home, you mention your mother has
a detailed book about Gil Albornoz.
I cartoon him in as some kind of handsome
fourteenth century Spanish "Cock Robin,"
some young Sir Robert Walpole type;
an intrepid papal general, statesman, legate,
committed to issuing the law code of the Marches
in Papal States. I'm more adept imagining
the Spanish boy in Luarca beside the sea.

•

In Orvieto, town of deep Etruscan reservoirs
(near the Fortezza Albornoz that is now
a public garden), built—like so many things
in Italy—in the time of the imperial papal world,
there are two distinct, winding stone passageways
in the curiously elegant Pozzo di San Patrizio.
Brick archways open into the hollow core
of the well. It is a place where, when we go,
in our modernity, we speak of world politics,
scientific laws, and enzymes. It is where,
with your help, I first began to grasp the Rosetta Stone
and your *tio abuelo's* work with the genetic code.

"All reactions are reversible." (Is it true
that inside of every rebel there is a dictator
trying to get out?) "Reversible phosphorylation ..."
(I have trouble keeping on the topic at hand;
"Ingredients and cooking," I tell myself)
"is a bacteria's recycling mechanism.
It's all about salvage, the bacteria
using the pathway to salvage Adenine."
(A dictatorship rising out of a republic?)
"They couldn't get anywhere with the commercially
available ADP, but the scavenging enzymes
showed up in the more amorphous *Azotobacter* glop.
It cleaved polynucleotides by phosphorolysis
rather than hydrolysis." (So much excitement
and pride in finding out about making things active
and inactive.) "... polynucleotide phosphorylase."

•

In 1975, for a 70th birthday tribute,
Salvador Dalí bestowed
his old schoolmate, Severo Ochoa,

a chain of five colorful,
winged nucleic acids.

•

Like Carmen, Severo's beloved wife,
I too had "coupled" into the fastidious
de Albornoz family. Severo was a tall,
courtly man used to opulence
and commanding courteous deference.
The first thing he said to me before
releasing my hand from our introductory
shake was, "What schools did you go to?"

And then there was that exacting
aristocratic, scientific, familial gaze.

Once, at a lull in a family lunch in a parador
in Toledo, where Severo had just been sharing
a story about riding a mule to a ridge
in Santorini, a woman approached
the table and asked for an autograph.

As soon as she withdrew, Severo turned
off the charm, turned back to me, and said,
in a fake American Midwestern accent, "Holy
Toledo! You'd think I was a football player!"

The rest of the lunch, I listened while he,
Carmen, and Jose (great-grandson of Manuel
de Albornoz), continued to speak in several
languages. Frequently, he turned and tenderly
translated lest I be left out of the conversation.

•

OCHOA CODA
In a photograph, Severo—gallant
and beaming in a white tie and tux—

dances at the Nobel gala.
Carmen smiles in his arms.

Frontera Sagrada

One should visit the Valley of the Fallen,
not because there is any reconciliation
to be found there. But to remind one's
self of the prisoners who lost their lives
quarrying the huge cavern, prisoners
whose names are not commemorated.

●

Eos: capricious; love; retribution
and cruelty memorialized in the sanctuary
of a grasshopper. Cursed to love
only a row of beautiful men.
To love someone as their youth fades,
as they fade, as they become
only a whisper. To be
commemorated on a vase or jug
while in a moment of mourning
or carrying away the beautiful body
of a maimed belovéd in a mysterious
field just before dawn.

                    Aurora:
first daughter; pagan goddess;
another de Albornoz.

●

Land of fans, clay roof tiles
and dancers heels on wooden floors,
lace, castles, and churches. Legacy
of Unamuno; Machado, García Lorca;
Jiménez, Bergamín.

●

In this fairytale, Maleficent is a dictator,
And the people of the kingdom
are spelled to a state of wakefulness.

Some, ultimately, will choose—
rather than exile—occupation
with its congealing frustrations

and risks; occupation, where praise—
in being both pointed and modest—
is an insinuating protest.

"Sometimes, one cannot simply
walk away." When Aurora chose
her final resting place, she turned

to the palm-covered island
where five hundred years earlier
the Church—in an awkward,

if not leaky craft, tendered
to land its story of Adam
and Eve. Upon leaving the walled

garden and facing the expedience
of labor, hadn't they taken with them
the volatile dream of Knowledge and Freedom?

Madrid, Please, Take Me; Be Mine

You are my flower,
My cork tree,
My honey bee.

You are my Istanbul,
My Venice,
My Granada.

My stealth maneuver,
My stormtrooper,
My armada.

My stormtrooper syndrome,
My Stockholm syndrome,
My savant.

You are my Ferdinand, my Egidio,
My Valentine. My Cardinal, my palace,
My fortress, my pre-Visigothic Iberian Law.

My churros and chocolate,
My ration of croquettes,
My Spanish tortilla,

My espresso,
My solo, my doble,
My café cortado.

You are my Castilian,
My Euskera, my Bable,
My Pig Latin.

You are my cold red
Apple, my old bota,
My glass of fresh water.

My Fountain of the Four Stations,
My Fountain of the Four Seasons,
My Fountain of the Conches,

My basin,
My fountain,
My statue.

My palisade, my walled garden,
My secret garden,
My paradise.

You are my spring of Parnassus,
My Fuente del Bruxo,
My hermitage, my hontanares.

My Café Gijón,
My Lhardy's,
My Los Palos.

My clubs,
My coins,
My swords.

You are my clean teacup,
My martini glass, my flute,
My grail, my chalice.

My true heart,
My red heart,
The ribs

Around
My own
Racing black heart.

Come be my Calle Méjico, my Atocha,
My Lavapiés, my Gran Vía.
Come be my Alcalá.

"Ángel Caído"
(Ricardo Bellver, El Retiro, Madrid, 1878)

Stunning to look at!
One bronze wing juts up
like the blade of a broken windmill fan.
Not Caravaggio's Saul, but a youth,
bound, crashing onto a stump:
a knee, an elbow, one hand raised.
Here, each Retiro sun, each full—
or nearly full—Retiro moon,
all the stars stand in
for the blinding, deafening,
clearly threatening might
that has forced the angel down.

•

The only statue of Lucifer in all of Europe.
In little more than half
a century, the notion
of the fallen
and the notion of a sole voice
resonate in new ways.

Found Painting, Found Poem

Like a serious piece of jewelry
glittering in a resort shop window

hawking its dazzle, this is neither
private lexicon nor hooligan of buzz

in free association. In nineteen thirty-six,
the German Luftwaffe bombed

the ancient Basque town of Guernica.
As commissioned, here, delivered

by a capable native son, is
ferocious monumentality. The killing

and maiming of several hundred
Spanish villagers was essentially done

for bombing practice, just like a lunatic
or self-promoting art vandal's desecrating

shenanigan: an indefensible target of deliberate
fascistic cruelty. "In love, there needs to be

two consenting people." When the painting
arrived in Madrid, we made a trip to see it.

It was installed in a huge bulletproof
glass cage in an annex of the Prado.

It was flanked by armed soldiers. We knew it
from the Museum of Modern Art in New York.

We had heard stories from our loved ones
who remembered seeing it in other venues.

What we saw was sad and shocking:
The picture looked forlorn, suffocated.

It was almost impossible to see.
That same summer, in a dark pool

of Parisian security, the "Mona Lisa"
also sadly seemed to float away from us.

●

Proximity is the cost, and virtue,
of a civil and democratic society.

We run the risk that some lunatic
or flashy self-promoter will violate

the public trust of an open space
because we value that space

as a democratic ideal.
Part of what's beautiful

about publicly displayed art,
aside from what's on display,

is that it implicates trust.
Standing beside art,

we represent respect
for a common welfare, civility.

Visiting Granada

Perhaps because my parents
made their livelihood tending plants
and animals, I have always been
grateful for each dish I have
since served or been served.

Down the road from where we lived
there was a man who was both
a plumber and an electrician.
He designed and installed
electric circuits and helped others
maintain their sinks and toilets.
The convenience of private water flow
efficiently tapped in the house
was a luxury no one took for granted.

Years later, I lived in Mojácar,
a remote and lovely Andalucían
village. Weekly, people
came to the local fountain
to draw and cart fresh water.

That same trip, visiting the Alhambra
and the lovely Albaicín of Granada,
I explored the mysterious eaves,
lattice screens, and pavilions
of the Abencerrajes. Prayers, salutations,
and lines of poetry sculpted in plaster
curled atop walls and over windows.

We wandered through the fountained
gardens, through the aesthetically
charged rooms beside the still pools
of Nasrid courts. We pondered the bloody
rivalries within the palatine ranks
and the intricate maintenance of such
a majestic medieval organization.

Later, that evening, friends and I
ate, walked arm-in-arm through
the small winding streets of the Albaicín.

Heading toward ice cream, we spoke
of the Spanish Civil War, of conflicts
in the world, of the disputed land
of Palestine. Finding our way around
the graffitied walls, we spoke of enduring
the discovery of the world's dangerous axis.

La Última Sombra ante la Ciudad

Here, the July sun anvils down
to the last shade before the medieval town.
The scruffy abandoned hill behind
the house we presently live in
(an ancient olive grove
and mill renovation), long ago,
was the original site of settlement
before today's nearby town.

Buses and cars slowly travel the new road
to shopping and executing business.
It angles up the nearby mountainside.
In the evenings, the gash becomes
a string of lights. The top of the mountain
disappears, and the lights along the road
become star points in a giant crown.

Bars across the brightly lit windows
of one of the houses by the side
of one of the smaller dusty roads
remind us that all intentional
trespasses—whether small
or international in scale—
are crimes of opportunity.

The hot summer afternoons are good
for little more than long siestas
and slow irrigations: cerveza,
tinto de verano, a granizado de limón.

Dogs, big dogs, little dogs,
find shade and nap.
When we have to be out
in the sun, we frequently
stop along the way
and catch our breaths
in whatever shade
there is to be found.

The Last Execution

We live in a two-story
house. *JULIAN GRIMAU*

APRIL 20, 1963
is scribbled

on a piece
of paper

upstairs. Downstairs,
you and I

scrabble and wonder
through the narrative:

torture, defenestration,
sentenced without due process

or deliberation, the deliberate
and nasty Caudillo,

the Keystone Kops fiasco
and tragedy of the firing squad.

Political Fallout
(For JLF, EL, & AMM)

What might be discerned from the faces
(the young girl, the three wordless boys)
in a book of Disfarmer photographs

before rushing out to meet you: three
other—were our families respectable
and Mexican—scorned "pochos,"
three tablemates who, like me,
have willed themselves across the miles
between this extravagant city
and a home of diminishing resources,
who, like me, have considerations
with translation—all that is worthy,
lost, resistant. Concerns about families
glimmering in the distance,
so many emigrants and *exiliados*
pushed or pulled on to greener pastures.

So many refugees. Hindi, Italian, Spanish,
American English. What do they speak
in Darfur? So many borders: Texas,
Northern Ireland, Palestine, a village
in Kargil. So many fresh, historical,
manmade and natural disasters.
"Oprah," opera, ETA.
The sincere dreams and trials
of different nations glint and flicker
for a moment in our conversation.
So few ways—and many of them
dangerous—to move ahead. Lamb
shank, ravioli, two plates of tagliata.

"Destino"

> "There are many advantages in puppets.
> They never argue. They have no crude views
> about art. They have no private lives."
> —Oscar Wilde

As the story goes in Spain—in Mojácar,
to be specific—Isabel Zamora,
a very young woman "in trouble,"
was bullied into a marriage and a move
to Chicago, where she allowed her son
to be adopted shortly after arriving.

"Destino," too, begins with a young woman
emerging from the edge of a near empty
landscape: ". . . my empty arms . . . my call."

The six-minute short follows
the love story of Chronos
and the ill-fated love
he has for a mortal. There is no
dialogue; the soundtrack features a song
by the Mexican composer Armando
Dominguez. The ballad's delicate sweeps
and lunges are performed by Dora Luz.
Every monument's inevitably
resistant to time. Notions
of love, fate, and death
float organically throughout the piece.

A moonbeam melts and runs
like molten metal; a hummingbird
drills a hole in the face of a wristwatch
where an artery should be; a hatch
of ants morphs into a landscape of bearded
bicyclists, an enormous peanut strapped
to the top of each rider's head.

The attention of Chronos's love
slithers into a shell, a garment,
embodies the shadow of a belfry's campana;
her head turns into dandelion pappus

and disperses into the wind
like notes from the tongue of a bell
or a flight of swallows.

A segment with a pair of tortoises
transporting two great stick puppets
collapses into the metaphor of baseball.

The miniature and the vast domains
of sheltered and unsheltered
melt into one another, availing
". . . my empty arms . . . my call,"

knelling "Destino," a call embodying
a shadow awaiting an echo

embodying a shadow of the monumental
in a destiny fulfilled—even one
in the most abandoned of places.

Self-evident

"If [we] don't invent a
new world, no one will."
> Nicolas Sarkozy,
> President of France,
> An address at Columbia University, 2010

A Commission

("The Martyrdom of St. Matthew," Caravaggio, 1599-1600)

A great and dark ambition
sought, wound, shoved its way through the streets
and police records of Rome. Howled, hurled
insults, hot artichokes, and stones would leave its signature
in blood, "Unloved, unlovely to look at,

I know I am alone." He waited,
like Matthew, for them to make their final choice,
for them to recognize the match. He waited,
like Saint Matthew must have, waited to be chosen,
waited for that final blow to come.

The French priests of San Luigi
dei Francesi already knew what they wanted:
no more delays, no more waiting
thirty years for something. He already knew what stood
at the center of one of the white canvases

even as he signed the contract,
"No hope. No fear." Later, scarlet would hemor-
rage across a somber floor, "I did this."
He would give them a silent painting burned blank
by passion, one clear and full of noise.

•

. . . No time for them to think.
Clearly, violence is usually outside
in the street—not in here. "Police! . . .
Someone, a sword!" A baptismal attendant has one
at his hip. But, it only incidentally

crosses another blade.
The bright and deathless light belongs outside
as if "In here, what does what we do have to do
with the time of day?" Except for Matthew and the straddling man,
they are used to continually seeking perfection.

They face each other. Seem
to choose each other. Their bare feet cross.
He surely has chosen Matthew, no one else.
Everyone else faces nothing. Now? . . . No, not just yet.
Matthew needs a moment to identify

what has been supplied.
White and deathless . . . is this the enemy? A trace
of pity: Can this be God? He has come before.
Another slender substitution? Matthew must
choose. No time to ask.

•

Ahead there is a frond,
of course, we know, but what of Matthew,
himself across the floor? What object
of contemplation did he choose? His assassin's body
as bright as a marble statue? His face,

that inevitable sword?
What is there for the screaming boy to turn to? What
besides all the backs and faces of these men,
all carelessly turning, so carefully paired?
Where can we get beneath the surface?

In the hollow mouth
of the noisy murderer or the desperate boy?
Alone, a quiet horror spreads from the wholeness
of Caravaggio's watching face. The Roman signatories
to the contract may have gotten

more than they expected.
At least, some of it, for now, we understand.
Any records making out the executioner?
The model? No. None other than what we see:
just a man hired to do the job.

Visit With an Old Model at Norwood
For Richard Howard

As you see, I'm
no longer able to stand alone,
          but, some nights I have a dream.
I stand, young and naked, in front of
          Fred's camera again.
                    Both my elbows
          extend overhead. A cuttlefish
                    swims by. I raise my face, and,
slowly, beginning with my eyes and feet, I
          dissolve into its
                    inky trail . . . .

                         O my . . .
          There I go again! Where were we . . . ? Yes.
                    Yes . . . . I've managed to pull a few
things together for you. Fred's parents. Yes,
          very nice looking.
                    They ran the tannery
          here at Norwood; they were well-to-do.
                    Victorians. Unitarians.
I remember them both very well; we
          called her *Lady Day*.

                    There should also be
          a photograph of Fred here . . . somewhere . . .
                    one of him back when he was
a little tyke. Here it is; yes, that's him. He
          couldn't have been more
                    than five or six when
          that was made. Cutie Patutie, all
                    ears and gray melancholy
eyes. Here's another that might interest you.
          I would call it
                    the Old Bullard Farm.
          You don't recognize it? Well, you've been
                    there. It's what you're calling

the Old Day Place. Yes; yes, it's always been
              a beautiful place. It
                            originally
              was an Edwardian house with
                     a mansard roof and shutters.
I can remember when they refurbished it,
              redid it Tudor
                            and equipped it
              with electricity and modern
                            conveniences. Let me see,
that would've been in '90 . . . or '91.

              These are a couple
                            of journals I used
              to subscribe to. Goodness! October,
                     1897. It
was the first one to pick up Fred.
              Interesting, isn't it?
                            As you can
              imagine, for those days it was . . . What
                            would be the word? . . . radical.
What did they go with? . . . *Ethiopian*.
              Suitable. The model
                            was Fred's chauffeur,
              Alfred Tanneyhill. Fred made some
                            astounding pictures of him.
What was it Fred called it? His . . . *African* . . . no—,
              Nubian—yes, yes,
                            that was it, his
              Nubian — Series. This ended up
                            in Stieglitz's collection. Let's
see: July, 1898. At one time,
              I had a print of this.
                            I thought it was
              really somethin'—the way his right arm
                            and left leg are like v's
going in opposite directions. May I? . . .
              For a moment . . .
                            Joseph Kiley (I
              have no idea who Mr. Kiley

is—or was) . . . "exquisitely
harmonious". . . . Here, Fred particularly
liked this part, "...In its
conception it is
distinctly Greek, indeed, it has but
one fault that I can mention:
the little ivory statuette is in
too high a key of
white for the subdued
tones of the balance of the picture."

Fred felt that photography
was a facing up or back to something,
a kind of facing
something divine.
A kind of "instancy of revelation"
he called it. And, boy,
did he ever know how to create a public
stir! You know he was
the first American
artist to ever exhibit a full
frontal nude. A sepia.
In Boston. I posed for it. It was a study
for the *Crucifixion*.
One critic said it
was "free of that look that makes most
photographs of this sort
merely indecent." Fred was interested in
presence. Oh, he was
interested in all
sorts of things. Your coming here today
has been such a pleasure. I
can't begin to tell you how delightful it
is to find someone
like you interested
in our . . . *explorations of originality*.
You could look up that sepia.
You may find . . . that you'll want to come visit
me again. But now,
if you'll excuse me,

I'd better get back to my place. I
imagine it's best before
dinner that I lie down awhile, rest these old
weary bones a spell.

Parajanov's "The Color of Pomegranates"

> "Sometimes the truth of a thing is not so much
> in the think of it, as in the feel of it."
> —Stanley Kubrick

Even in
this world

of lice, dogma,
and multiple possibilities,

absence is built in.
Sadly, we live

without the stain
of your "Hiawatha"

or your "Faust."
Rest in peace.

You leave us
to argue lace:

whether—or
most likely not—

the fate of the poet
is as important

as the poems
themselves.

What Hitchcock Was After

Hitchcock wanted
Montgomery Clift

to inhabit one
of the young

wayward killers
in "Rope."

And for the role
of the sharp-eyed

prep school master
(which went to Jimmy

Stewart), Hitchcock's
choice was Cary Grant.

What is in the can
is in the can.

What is in the box
is in the box.

I Shall Not Want

Because I was the child
of a cowboy. Because

my mother was diagnosed
with polio two days after I

was born. Because my four-year-old
sister managed to bundle me up,

put me in the little red wagon,
pull me out to the old Ford

(a metal visor gusseted
above its windshield),

open its door, and waggle
me onto one of its seats.

(I am not exactly sure who
wrangled my impetuous

two-year-old brother.) Town
was a county dirt road drive away.

My mother hobbled to the car
using a pair of high-back chairs

as crutches. Because my nearly
unstoppable mother—herself

raised in the country
and an only child—still drove,

her three fledglings
satellited around her.

Others—out of our necessity
and their kindness—would

carry me. Years later,
we lost her parents,

my brother, sister,
dad, one at a time.

Because I took to calling
Mother by the name

of each relationship we'd lost:
Joyce, Jack, Mother, Sweetheart.

Each Christmas eve,
we commemorate our losses

by calling out our loved ones'
names and respectively

tossing a firecracker
into the trunk

of the old hollow tree.
My stooped mother—absolute

in her pedigree and her perspective—
and I come back to the familiar ear:

my mother, to murmur
something else insistent

that she has remembered
about stewardship or gratitude,

or about the resilience of love,
me, to burble and amble on

about metastasizing
prickly pear, worn-out wells

and gates, about fences,
and pastures

of dark invading cedars
and thirsty cattle.

Turtle Bay, Deutal Bay
(For Giovanni Mastrogiacomo)

Another walk in the U.N. rose garden
affords a view of the river, and another glance
at the statue of a man hammering a sword
into a plowshare. Our conversations have settled
increasingly on two concerns—Europe's wobble

toward a transparent and unifying constitution
—and your ache of singularity. Today an island
in the current of Hart Crane's river still beckons
as it did when Poe "bathed" here. (A few decades
later, a battery of slaughterhouses would choke

these banks.) It might entice as a goal for an invigorating
swim, but, today, Turtle Bay's tricky currents churn
with representative numbers, the international
debts of European nations, and my attempting
to muster enough fraternal intimacy to keep you—

bureaucrat and friend—afloat. When you tell
of how the requests for manifests and forward-
moving policies in multiple languages
nearly exhausts, I tell you of a friend
who has emailed me the pleasure

of her anachronistic thoughts: Jefferson
reading the soliloquies of Dickinson—
relating to her admonition and seclusion—
"Unto my Books—so good to turn—
Far ends of tired Days—".

"Follies"

December, 1971. A light snow. The Taft Hotel.
Our room across the street, overlooked
the Winter Garden stage door. I was green
and this was to be my first taste of Broadway.
By the time the lights and trumpets

lifted on the "Loveland" number,
I was lost in years monogrammed
across silk sashes, wigs, and in the follies
of relationships—only a few going right.
Are we ever awake, or is all of this dream?

Not a tiny fleck of foreshadowing that,
given a handful of years and a little
more seasoning, this would become
my home, the anvil of my art, the abode
of *my* glorious ghosts for over thirty years.

2011, primed with anticipation and an
entirely new gaggle of friends, I rustle
in my seat through "the revival"—cast,
lose, and reel myself back in; once again
in the bars of ". . . spend sleepless nights . . . ."

Wilde and Genet Bequeathed

a hemi-quadriga—
two—of whatever

they were . . . two-bit
peg boys, a slightly

more seasoned chicken
and his mate, artists who opted

to work in a house rather than
sail away and grub for blubber,

or two provincial boys
with an innate sense

of the parameters
of their ethereal voices

and the tender limits
of service or local

glamour, the charade,
the harshness of the trap

or team, two squeaky
boys by greatness

in the indelible posture
of Claire and Solange,

Blanche and Stanley,
George and Martha,

or one in the guise
of Cleopatra, Ophelia,

"Kitty Litter,"
"Thea Uther Bolyn,"

Irma, Violet, Delilah,
rhapsodic Salome.

Identity Redux
("Paved Paradise," John Kelly, 2009)

> "The first television program put
> into reruns was "The Lone Ranger."
> Snapple bottle top

A frame. Two keyboards, a bass,
a dulcimer, and five guitars
set the stage for "Dagmar Onassis."
Kiss. Kiss. What? Has it been
sixteen years? What does
it matter that the roses upstage
on the grand piano are red?

If you have been asked
to wear the dream,
what difference does it matter
if the dress is white or blue
and the shoes shine red? We park
the day's carousel
and heed whatever
falls out and captivates.

With ghosts—Damia? Hutch?
Jacques Brel? Judy
Garland?—shimmering
somewhere nearby—the evening
nears its end: John Kelly's guitars
and Joni Mitchell's plaintive
melodies about longing, sex,
our Frankenstein technologies,
Science's tunnel vision.
Tunnel vision.

The wingless moon floats
beyond the encapsulating
spotlight, and each one
in the theater must find
each's own way home.

Notes

Walking at the U.N.
"Poetry does not need to commit itself politically to be political. On the contrary, it is precisely when it commits itself politically that it ceases to be both politics and poetry, ceases to be the politics of poetry. If every great poetry is political, it is so by definition, since it seeks a foundation for the commonwealth in the truth of the heart, guaranteed and restored through the integrity of language." ("The Poet and the King," a study about Jean de La Fontaine, a French poet at the time of Louis the XIV by Marc Fumaroli, translated by Jane Marie Todd, p. 15)

Platée
Rameau's first attempt at comic opera. The plot concerns an ugly water nymph who believes that Jupiter the king of the gods, is in love with her. The work was initially called a *ballet bouffon*, though it was later styled a *comédie lyrique*.

It was written for the celebrations of the wedding of Louis, Dauphin of France, son of King Louis XV of France, to the Infanta Maria Theresa of Spain.

Le Soldat Avec Les Besoins Infantiles
(The Soldier with Infantile Desires) From the fourth stanza on, the poem is a dramatic monologue in the voice of the female fairy addressed in Keats's "La Belle Dame Sans Merci."

Noblesse Oblige, Before The Mirror
pavos reales—(Spanish) peacocks
paons—(French) peacocks
redingote—outer riding coat

Noble Chart, A Radiance – 1794
Antoine Laurent Lavoisier, a French nobleman, is heralded as the father of modern chemistry.

Lavoisier, who briefly had served as a minor tax collector, was guillotined. He was only fifty-years-old. Isaac Asimov references his execution as "the most deplorable single casualty of the revolution."

"You are using for the defence precisely the same weapons which were once used for the attack." Lavoisier to Edward King.

In 1780, Lavoisier blackballed Jean-Paul Marat, a journalist who "fancied himself a scientist," when the latter applied for membership in the French Academy of Sciences. Marat never forgot nor forgave this act of Lavoisier. Both Marat and Lavoisier would be subjects for paintings by Jacques-Louis David.

Baudelaire in 1846 wrote of David's painting, "The Death of Marat": "Where is the ugliness that hallowed Death erased so quickly with the tip of his wing? Now Marat can challenge Apollo. He has been kissed by the loving lips of Death and he rests in the peace of his metamorphosis."

Royalties
From the lyrics of "La Boheme":
"Una terribil tosse l'esil petto le scuote . . ."
　　　"A terrible cough makes her tiny breast tremble. . ."
"Te lo rammenti quando sono entrata la prima volta, la?"
　　　"Do you remember when I first came in here?"
"Soli. . . . d'inverno e cosa da morire!"
　　　"Alone . . . in winter and a thing might kill you!"

Lutece
sillion—shiny gash of earth made by a plow

Cecelia Gallerani—the young woman who modeled for Leonardo da Vinci's painting *The Lady with an Ermine.* Neither rich nor noble, she was betrothed at ten years to a young nobleman of the house of Visconti but the marriage was called off. Cecelia, renowned for her beauty, her scholarship, and her poetry, became the mistress of Lodovico Sforza, Duke of Milan. Hers was the first salon in Europe.

H5N1, also known as bird flu, is a subtype of the influenza A virus. In 2011 virologist Ron Fouchier, in a lab transformed the virus into the supergerm of virologists' nightmares, enabling it to spread from one animal to another through the air. The work was done in ferrets, which catch flu the same way people do and are considered the best model for studying it.

Jules Leotard—a famous French trapeze artist

Lutetia non urbus, sed orbis. (Latin) Paris is not an urban center, it is a universe.

cephalophore—a saint who is generally depicted carrying his or her own head

St. Denis—home to the royal necropolis of France and the place of queens' coronations

The Afternoon of Infant Gods
The notion of a boy who would never grow up was based on James M. Barrie's older brother who died in an ice-skating accident the day before he turned 14, and thus always stayed a young boy in his mother's mind.

However, James Barrie publicly identified Peter Llewelyn Davies as the source of the name for the title character in his famous play. This public identification as "the original Peter Pan" plagued Davies throughout his life, which ended in suicide.

Plaza de la Encarnación, Seville
"You have not abandoned me!" ("No me ha dejado.") or "She [the city] has not abandoned me [the king]."
The motto, according to one legend, refers to the city's support of King Alphonse X in a 13th-century war with his son, Don Sancho. Another places the phrase in the mouth of Ferdinand III while riding into the city after expelling the Moors in 1248. This motto is seen in the city flag and throughout Seville, inscribed on manhole covers and on some street signs.

Victoria Kent
The first woman to become a lawyer in Spain and a Republican

politician noted for prison reform. In 1930 she came to fame for defending—at a court martial—Álvaro de Albornoz for his part in the revolutionary uprising of December 1930. (De Albornoz would shortly afterwards go on to become minister of justice and later the future president of the Republican government in exile.)

Kent served as the Director of Prisons 1931-32 and was responsible for introducing enlightened prison reform, including the abolition of the ball and chain for prisoner restraint. Kent (1898-1987) lived in exile in Paris. Later taught in Mexico and died in the United States.

At Every "Tosca"
Álvaro de Albornoz Liminiana was a political reformer and champion of the secular constitutional state of Spain. After serving as Minister of Justice and President of the Republican Government in exile, de Albornoz died in exile in Mexico, Oct. 22, 1954 survived by his wife (Amalia Salas) and two children (Concha and Alvarito).

A Life Facing the Sea
POLYNUCLEOTIDE PHOSPHOROLYSIS
A method of synthesizing high molecular weight RNA-like polynucleotides outside the cell. The chance discovery of this process in 1955 proved to be the cited basis of Ochoa's Nobel Prize Award four years later.

Frontera Sagrada
Aurora de Albornoz (January 22, 1926–June 6, 1990) was born in Luarca, Asturias, Spain. As a youth, she lived in Luarca with her parents, sister, and extended family, throughout the Spanish Civil War, 1936 to 1939—an event that informed her later poetry.

Madrid, Please Take Me; Be Mine
This was written as a valentine for Jose Fernandez, nephew of Aurora de Albornoz. Written after reading Catherine Bowman's poem "I Want to Be Your Shoebox."

Found Painting, Found Poem
8th stanza quote: Agnes Tricoire (lawyer for the owner of a vandalized painting by Cy Twombly).

On April 26, 1937, during the Spanish Civil War, twenty-eight Nazi German bombers undertook an aerial attack of the Basque town of Guernica, Spain. The Spanish government commissioned Pablo Picasso to paint a large mural for the Spanish display at the Paris International Exposition (the 1937 World's Fair in Paris). The Guernica bombing inspired Picasso. Within 15 days of the attack, Pablo Picasso began painting this mural. On completion, Guernica was displayed around the world. For many years it was in New York City. As of 1981 it has hung in Madrid.

Italics: Michael Kimmelman, "Abroad, A Symbol of Freedom and a Target for Terrorists," *The New York Times*, Oct. 13, 2007.

Visit with an Old Model at Norwood
F. Holland Day was the first fine art photographer in America to include in a public exhibit a print of a full frontal male nude ("Study for the Crucifixion," March 1898, Boston).

Parajanov's "The Color of Pomegranates"
Sergei Parajanov (1924-1990) was a Soviet-Armenian filmmaker. Besides the extraordinary films and biography of Parajanov, one could read Joanne Nucho's 2004 essay "Deep Red."

What Hitchcock Was After
Look at how many of Cary Grant's film titles play off of a closety or gay suggestion: "I'm No Angel," "Born to Be Bad," "Topper," "The Awful Truth," "In Name Only," "Suspicion," "Notorious," "I Was a Male War Bride," "Crisis," "People Will Talk," "Monkey Business," "Indiscreet," and "Charade."

Turtle Bay, Deutal Bay
The Dutch governor of New York granted a 40-acre manor known as Deutal Bay Farm to two Englishmen in 1639. "Deutal" was used to describe the supposed shape of the bay. The phrase is Dutch for "bent blade." It would appear that "deutal"

eventually gave way to the English word "turtle." The U.N. building now stands in the space the bay once occupied. The neighborhood is now called Turtle Bay.

"Follies"

Calderón de la Barca:
"¡Que toda la vida es sueño,
y los sueños, sueños son!"
Translation:
"For all of life is a dream,
And dreams, are nothing but dreams."

Acknowledgments

Grateful acknowledgement is made to the editors of the following publications in which these poems first appeared, sometimes in earlier versions:

Chelsea: "The Bath Scene in 'Gattopardo'"

Commonweal Magazine: "Plaza de la Encarnación, Seville"

Connotation: "'Platée'" and ""Ángel Caído""

Fogged Clarity: "Dixie Queen" "Follies" "Identity Redux" "Noble Chart, A Radiance – 1794" and "The Zeppelin Field at Nürnberg"

Ganymede: "Liu's Executioner"

Guernica: "Victoria Kent"

Harvard Review: "Le Soldat Avec Les Besoins Infantiles"

The Journal: "Madrid, Please, Take Me; Be Mine"

Lodestar: "Visit with an Old Model at Norwood"

New England Review: "Self-Evident"

Ocho: "Wilde and Genet Bequeathed"

Ocean State Review: "Noblesse Oblige, Before the Mirror"

Ploughshares: "Beauty"

Silk Road: "Frontera Sagrada"

VIA: Voices in Italian America: "A Commission"

•

Center for Book Arts: "Reading : Writing" – Letterpress Broadside (edition of 100, Sarah Nicholls)

la contemplación de la impureza (Tres en Suma Madrid, Dec. 2009): "Victoria Kent" and "Imperial Carpet" (with Spanish translations by Natalia Carbajosa)

Barrow Street Poetry

Self-evident
Scott Hightower (2012)

Emblem
Richard Hoffman (2011)

Mechanical Fireflies
Doug Ramspeck (2011)

Warranty in Zulu
Matthew Gavin Frank (2010)

Heterotopia
Lesley Wheeler (2010)

This Noisy Egg
Nicole Walker (2010)

Black Leapt In
Chris Forhan (2009)

Boy with Flowers
Ely Shipley (2008)

Gold Star Road
Richard Hoffman (2007)

Hidden Sequel
Stan Sanvel Rubin (2006)

Annus Mirabilis
Sally Ball (2005)

A Hat on the Bed
Christine Scanlon (2004)

Hiatus
Evelyn Reilly (2004)

3.14159+
Lois Hirshkowitz (2004)

Selah
Joshua Corey (2003)